# THE WINNING PHYSIQUE

## How to Get the Competitive Edge on Stage

by

**Claire Johnson**

THE NAKED WARRIOR

The Winning Physique
First published in 2014
Copyright © 2014 by i-Jolly Publishing

2nd Edition
**ISBN:** 9798559441924
**Imprint:** Independently published

# ABOUT THE AUTHOR

## Claire Johnson

I am the CEO of The Naked Warrior which delivers 3 winning online coaching programs and Founder of The Naked Warrior Tribe online community plus author of two books - The Winning Formula :Discover the Secrets to Unleash Your Alphafemale and this, The Winning Physique: How to Get the Competitive Edge on Stage.

I am a leading female mindset, nutrition and training coach and through my coaching programs I empower women to lose the mental junk holding themselves back plus identify their triggers and self-sabotage habits so they can create strategies to achieve success and their desired results.

I have created an online Facebook community called The Naked Warrior Tribe which is for women who are looking to stop letting self-doubt, criticism and negative self-talk hold them back from achieving their desired results with their health, fitness, body and mindset so they feel energised and confident on a daily basis leaving a positive impact on those around them.
Join the tribe to stop letting self-doubt, criticism and negative self-talk hold you back from achieving their desired results with their health, fitness, body and mindset and feel energised and confident daily!

Having worked health and fitness industry, across a few continents, providing nutrition, training and coaching programs to individuals and groups since 2002 as well as educating and teaching those wanting a career in fitness, Claire is currently based in the UK, is a huge aerial fitness fan and mum.

I am also an online health coach, personal trainer and also group exercise instructor plus the author of The Winning Formula and The Winning Physique and have regularly contributed articles and blogs to publications such as Oxygen, Clean Eating, Marie Claire and online to Essex Baby. I have also created and presented an online TV channel for Australia and NZ's largest Personal Training Franchise. I have competed as both a figure and bikini competitor at city, state and national level with 1st place and top 3 wins.

Find out more about my successful female empowerment coaching programs or work on a one to one basis by contacting me cj@thenakedwarrior.co.uk, check out my website www.thenakedwarrior.co.uk, or follow me on socials by searching thenakedwarrior.

*"Whilst in Australia I embarked on my journey into the world of body sculpting, competing at State and National levels. The experiences I went through have driven me to educate females on how to get in competition shape without feeling restricted or deprived, I'm extremely passionate about wanting to show you how, with whole foods, smart training and rest, competing can be one of the greatest experiences of your life."*

**Competition History**
June 2012
INBA City Nationals – Open Figure 2nd
INBA All Female Classic – Open Figure 4th
May 2012
ANB South Coast – Open Figure 4th
Sept 2010
INBA NSW Titles – Sports Model 30+ – 3rd
May 2010

INBA Sydney Titles  – Tall Figure 1st
WNBF Sydney Titles  – Novice Figure 1st
ANB Sydney Titles – Open Figure 5th
May 2009
INBA Sydney Titles  – Tall Figure 2nd
ANB South Coast Titles  – Novice Figure 4th
ANB Sydney Titles – Tall Figure 3rd

# CONTENTS

# CJ's Top Tips
# How to be a Successful Sports Model
# & Figure Competitor

## Your guide from the experts on how to get ahead of the game

Welcome to the wonderful world of female physique sculpting, the broad term that incorporates categories such as figure, physique and female bodybuilding plus sports, bikini and fitness model.

To be reading this you may already be part of this sometimes controversy and confusing world or looking to learn more about what it takes to step up on stage in front of an auditorium full of spectators.

The wonderful world of competing is complex and to those on the outside it can seem unhealthy, obsessive, extremist and downright weird! There seems to be an array of negative perceptions which are unwarranted and can make it even more daunting to a new person to try. An experienced competitor can find themselves on the receiving end of negative comments which create unnecessary challenges. There is a minefield of conflicting information about how to diet, train and become stage ready and ultimately we all want to know how to present the best possible package to the judges. Some programs say to eat one thing whilst another steers well clear, plus with conflicting information about training, posing, supplements and words thrown around such as dehydration, starvation and post comp blow out the very thought of competing itself is extremely overwhelming.

Many females dream of stepping on stage, to feel the sense of accomplishment and pride as well as creating their ultimate body yet are unsure of where to start as well as what is involved. The feeling of achievement when you set your mind to something, to really go out and grab it with both hands is amazing and this is why so many ladies choose to give it a go. Competing empowers women, not just during the comp prep phase but also on competition day. It is the self-confidence and life lessons you learn along the way that you take away with you when stepping off stage that roll over into all aspects of your life to truly enhance it.

You only have to walk into any newsagent to see the array of magazines with a range of looks that are sold as being inspirational. If you switch on the T.V. or surf the internet you are bombarded with images of wafer thin models being portrayed as the epitome of beauty who have the perfect body. Even in the celebrity world you can't win, you are condemned for being too thin or too fat or too this or too that! Jeez!

With so much pressure from media and society I truly believe that females need to build their self-confidence and own inner beauty to rise above the barrage of images that can lead to negative feelings and low self-worth. The best way for girls to empower themselves and love the skin they are in is to be healthy, strong and active. To sculpt the ideal body females need to weight train as well as eat clean unprocessed food. Forget hammering yourself with constant cardio to change your body and create your competition body, the key is really to work with resistance.

So why should you train with weights? The most important reason is to build and maintain muscle. The more muscle you have the greater your capacity to store carbohydrates so you no longer have to be low-carb! Building more muscle is the key element to revving up your metabolism and creating shape to your body. The process of lifting weights puts stress on the muscles so that the body responds to compensate for the new loads being placed upon them. This muscle requires energy – hence your tight toned body has the capacity to burn more calories. Muscle is denser than fat and as you begin to build more you may notice that your weight doesn't change too much yet you are getting smaller and clothes are getting looser. This is what actually happens when women weight train, it is a myth that we start to get bulky and masculine. So rather than worrying about what the scales say, go with how you look and feel, be comfortable being 1 or 2kgs heavier and being 1 or 2 dress sizes smaller.

By choosing to live actively and increasing your knowledge on what to eat you can truly take control of your own health and fitness goals so that you do not succumb to feelings of self-doubt.

The competitor journey can start off by simply making this choice, without any intention to compete and get on stage. Most competitors find they love the results they see and want to take it to the next level. When you start exercising regularly and eating healthy clean wholesome food you are actually laying the foundations to make your competitor prep phase easier. If you have already created habits that are like second nature then when you have to ramp it up a gear, the transition is seamless and easier to integrate into your current lifestyle.

Even if you do not wish to compete, do not underestimate the power of learning self-discipline in conjunction with an increased focus on your own health and fitness. By feeling more secure in your body this allows natural self-confidence to grow from within. This in turn leads to happiness and personal satisfaction. So learn to become comfortable in your own skin regardless of if you want to compete or not.

My own journey started with a small niggle of desire and a wanting to do something different. I wanted to test my capabilities and see what I was made of mentally as well as find out how to transform my body physically. I had always admired strong women who had presence that oozed an inner confidence, and yes I was one of those girls who regularly flicked through fitness magazines wishing that it was me in the magazine and wondering if I could look like them.

I thought to myself one day that will be me and told others around me that someday I would do a competition. I then decided to do a comp before I turned 30 and as the impending milestone was just 6 months away, the pivotal decision was made and locked in! The 'gonna', 'wanna' and 'someday' turned into 'this is it I am doing'.

Did I know what I was about to do - no. Was I ready for the process - no. Was I scared and apprehensive - of course! Was I willing to do whatever it takes - you bet I was and I am so grateful I had the guts to take the plunge and just give it a go. I had nothing to lose (apart from a few kgs!) and I was ready to see what I could do. I cannot express in words what I learnt from the experience, not only about training and nutrition plus of course the wonderful world of competing, but it was what I had learnt about me that was the greatest gift. Yes it was life changing, my belief in my ability and willingness to try new things just sky rocketed. I learnt the power of goal setting, commitment and discipline as well as how to be in control of my mind and body. It wasn't all plain sailing and I was very lucky and fortunate to have a close knit network of support to help through the highs and lows. The light at the end of the tunnel truly does shine bright.

I love the sport for the increased mental strength, self-assuredness and happiness it brings you. I love the excitement at the start of a comp prep, I love the progression you see from your commitment in the off season as each competition gets closer. I love seeing old friends again on competition day as well as the camaraderie and girl power spirit backstage and I love the feeling of walking out into those bright lights and showing off your hard work and commitment. I also love stepping off stage and getting back into normal life!

One of the reasons for bringing this book together is to show girls that competing doesn't have to be scary, that it can be fun and with a little bit of persistence, determination plus some small sacrifices, amazing achievements are possible.

I want to help overthrow the negative perceptions that competing is unhealthy and damaging for your body and show how to get up on stage, regardless of which category you do in the healthiest possible way.

I have brought together an inspirational group of ladies who all have the same passion and desires, yet with different backgrounds, to share their stories on how they got into competing. I hope by reading this collection of extraordinary stories told by ordinary girls who simply ignited a spark inside them to pursue their passion that you too can be empowered to take the next step.

You can then make a fully informed decision on whether or not you want to get up on stage or just start living a healthier life. Regardless of how much information you read or how many shows you watch, I can guarantee the greatest learning experience is in just doing it, so instead of telling yourself you can't do it, why not tell yourself you can? The backbone to any successful journey is trusting you are on the right path and having faith in yourself.

# *Lindy Olsen*

*Lindy Olsen needs no introduction; she is iconic, influential and has an incredibly huge passion for wanting to give back to others so that they believe in themselves. Lindy is an inspiration who provides support, knowledge and experience to so many. I have never met anyone who has a bad word to say about her. She has contributed so much to this sport plus positively influenced so many females across all walks of life.*

*It was a privilege to interview Lindy, her enthusiasm and honesty demonstrates how grounded and true to purpose she really is. I am honored to welcome and introduce Lindy and have her share her story with you.*

**CJ: Lindy, you have achieved phenomenal success and are role model to so many people, can you share how this incredible journey began?**

Believe it or not I used to be a lazy, comfortable size 14, I was the fat girl at the beach in board shorts who had tried every diet to lose weight. You name it, I tried it! I hated the gym as it represented everything I wasn't. It was not until one night at a dinner with friends that I was convinced to go try this gym out whilst Dallas (husband) was away working overseas. For me this was about getting healthy and there was no inclination to compete.

**CJ: Can you remember the feeling as you entered the gym?**

Yes, I actually walked out! I remember walking up the stairs and seeing all these amazing physiques, it was a gym full of competitors like something out of a Rocky movie so I actually turned around and walked back down the stairs. Luckily this old guy saw who came running after me and asked me to come back. He actually met me half way down the stairs and his exact words were "Don't worry baby we will look after you. We will make this work and we will believe in you until you believe in yourself."

**CJ: Wow, that is incredible – was it this reassurance that helped get you started?**

I will never forget that moment as it provides the foundation of my passion and is the basis for what drives me now. I want to be able to provide the same amount of inspiration and hope to someone to be able to feel great about themself like I was given back then.

**CJ: So how did you go from this moment on the stairs to deciding to compete?**

Well within the first two weeks of going there I noticed that I felt different, I had more energy and thought "yep, there is something to this!" It was around the 4 month mark that I was approached to compete and at first I was very resistant. It was the era when you had to wear a G-string on stage and I was the board short girl, not a G-string wearing one! How could I go from the fat girl on the beach to baring my bum on stage!

I was told they would put me on a competition diet and train me. I was weight training 4 times a week as well as completing a 45 min walk every day so 5 ½ months later I found I had lost 29kgs! I was on my own during my very first comp prep and it was the support and belief that I got from my coach that kept me going. Dallas came home from overseas and found a shredded wife – he was so proud of me.

**CJ: I'm sure he was also very surprised! Tell us about your first show?**

The morning of the show I woke up scared shitless! I had no idea what to expect, I felt unprepared I couldn't pose properly - plus I was told that I would be put straight into the open category!

So I pumped up back stage, put my bikini on and then literally froze – I was so petrified I could not move and it took a good friend of mine to literally push me out onto the stage. As soon as I was out there and I saw the lights I became someone else, it was like I transformed into an actress and started acting out the role of doing my thing. I can clearly remember the moment when we were told to turn and face the rear – this was such a nerve wracking moment as I was about to show my bum off!

**CJ: You actually won your first show too, that must have been such a surreal feeling?**

Yes I won the open and I won the overall, I really could not believe that I had won, there were definitely tears and it was this feeling of accomplishment that drove me to continue competing.

**CJ: Like many who compete for the first time, you were hooked! How were the next few years for you?**

Well I stayed with the same coach for the next 3 years and each time I got ready for a show I found I had to do more cardio and eat less – I was literally starved into each competition. I was following a plan that is the complete opposite of what I do know. Unfortunately I learnt the hard way what such a restrictive diet does, which not only completely stress my body and impacted my hormones but I found that I just couldn't get lean anymore. I started to research more to find a better solution – this is something that I would recommend to everyone interested in competing. You need to empower yourself with knowledge and you should research your coach and the sport.

**CJ: What was different with your new coach's approach?**

I found a very experienced coach where no foods were cut out. Programs were designed to maximise metabolism and health. I learnt there is no reason why competing should damage your metabolism and as I was able to heal myself I decided that I wanted to compete again.

**CJ: This new method that you learnt formed the basis of your 7 Rules of Success – can you share those with us?**

Sure, these are the basic rules I follow every single day.

1. ALWAYS eat a LEAN source of protein at EVERY meal!
2. Always eat 5-7 meals EVERY day about 3-4 hours apart
3. Eat your greens…
4. Every 9 out of 10 meals you have, has to be in your plan.
5. AVOID sugar and limit your complex carbs with your last two meals unless you are active at night!
6. Drink at least 500ml of water for every 10 kg of body weight
7. Move more!

More details on each of these rules can be found on Lindy's website - www.lindyolsen.com

**CJ: Do you follow these in the off season and during comp prep?**

Yes absolutely – there is no cutting of any macronutrient, I eat from all food groups, including dairy! If anything, during comp prep I increase my portion sizes and will eat up to a kg of veges a day! I keep eating good fats as well as keep a treat meal too! The only thing that is reduced is the portion size of the treat meal. There is also no off and on season, this doesn't exist for me. If I want to tighten up for a photoshoot then I add an extra walk on the weekend and follow the rules really strictly. For instance I would have a treat every second day rather than every day.

**CJ: And you followed these principles whilst achieving phenomenal success so they clearly work.**

I have been a very lucky girl, I don't have the best shape and genetics yet I have learnt to work to my strengths. It is hard work and determination that has helped me achieve what I have. I make sure that I out work the competition – sure if someone has better genetics they will most likely beat me. What I lack genetically I make up for with heart! It is so much sweeter and more rewarding to see someone kick arse on stage who has not achieved the look easily over someone with great genetics.

**CJ: What about training, how is that structured?**

I do 4 hours of weight training a week plus walk every day. I never run, I never do intervals. Closer to a competition I will increase my cardio to twice a day, 45 minutes each time.

**CJ: You are an inspiration for so many, can you share what motivates you and keeps you focused?**

My drive comes from wanting to be a great role model and be an example for what is possible. This sport is all about making small improvements and being a better version of you. I feel that you can always improve, whether it be physically, emotionally and even spiritually and the journey to be a better me in all these areas will drive me forever.

I want to show that if you eliminate all excuses then anything is possible. When I was preparing for the 2010 show I wrote "This is the one" on a post it note and kept looking at it anytime I needed a boost.

**CJ: Let's talk about 2010, this was your first Pro Show and you won both Pro Women's Figure and Pro Women's Muscle**

Yes, in 2010 I felt that my mind and body was the best it had ever been and I was so happy as I felt I had finally made it, I had achieved my ultimate dream and reached the pinnacle of my sport.

**CJ: That is such an amazing achievement, how does this impact you when you return to normal life after such a big show?**

Well I actually fell into a 6 month depression after this, I felt lost and did not know where to go after this dream was achieved. It took me ten years to get here, I had finally got a pro world title and I didn't know where to go next. I thought now who am I? If I am no longer striving for a pro title then what do I do?

**CJ: So how did you come back from this feeling?**

It was difficult to deal with at first and then I focused on realigning my priorities and really evaluate what I want from life. I have achieved what I want physically from life and now I am focusing on my spiritual and emotional sides. Plus I want to help others not settle for being average, I want to empower them to choose to be better, in all areas and show them it is simply a choice.

**CJ: What is your advice to others to combat the post comp blues?**

You need to work out what is truly important to you and until you do you will still go through the internal struggles. Understand why you chose to compete in the first place plus know what is important to you for the rest of your life outside of competing as this is what will motivate you to move forward. Try not to base your identity on a show.

You need to give yourself another challenge, ask yourself what else do you want to achieve? This will give you your identity and when you create a plan then follow it you will become powerful beyond any measure. You will know in your gut that where you are going is the right track for you and this will keep you doing whatever you need to do to get it done.

**CJ: Great advice Lindy, do you have any other pearls of wisdom?**

Absolutely! My number one top tip is believe you can and you will! Don't let anyone else determine what you are capable of and never limit yourself. If you believe your dreams are possible and then try, really try with everything you have, and stay determined you cannot fail. Too many people let themselves get in the way and let negative self talk hold them back. Plenty of people start, yet give up too easily and if you truly give everything you can't fail. Fear is what holds people back so become fearless.

I always say to stay true to yourself, don't be anyone else, just be the best version of you. That's all you can control. Don't be a diva, keep your attitude in check and if your focus is always on your improvements then you have already won.

**CJ: Powerful statements! I am pumped and inspired hearing that. Lindy, do you look to anyone for your inspiration?**

I don't follow anyone as I find this leads to comparing and judging yourself. My inspiration comes from those around me, those who have helped me to understand me so I can be better.

Having Greg Dolman as my trainer and mentor has taught me to trust myself and believe in me. Greg has helped in telling myself "I can do it" and allow myself to live in the now and to go for it every single day.

People who live in their truth, who are honest, genuine and have integrity are inspiring as are those who have overcome adversity, got out of their comfort zones or faced their fears.

**CJ: So what is next on your agenda – where to from here?**
I am not sure if I will compete again, my focus for now is to help others increase their self-belief and give them hope. Who knows though, maybe if I have a family I will get back on stage afterwards – just to prove to anyone who says it can be done that it actually can!

**CJ: I love that, you always strive to open people's minds. Is there anything else you would like to share?**

I would just like to say a huge thank you to all the people I have met along the way. I am truly grateful for what I have been taught and have learnt that good things happen to good people.

**CJ: Thank you so much for your time, your inspiration and your passion!**

## Competition History

2010
WSNO/FAME USA World Titles
1st Place - Pro Women's Figure Class
1st Place - Pro Women's Muscle Model
2007
WSNO/FAME USA World Titles
1st Place - Open Women's Figure Class (Offered Pro Card) 1st
Place - Open Women's Muscle Model (Offered Pro Card)
NBA/PNBA USA International Flex Appeal All Female
Championships
 1st Place - Open Women's Figure (USA Physique)
2006
NABBA/WFF Commonwealth Titles
2nd Place - Open Women's Figure Class (Tall Division)
2005
WFF Victorian Championships
1st Place - Open Women's Figure Class (Tall Division)
WFF Southern Hemisphere Championships
1st Place - Open Women's Figure Class (Tall Division)
WFF Universe Championships (Germany 10/06/2005)
4th Place - Women's Performance Over 30
2004
INBA World All Female Muscle and Fitness Classic 1st Place -
Women's Open Figure Champion (Tall Division)
2003
INBA Victorian Championships
1st Place - Open Women's Figure Class (Tall Division) OVERALL
MS FIGURE VICTORIAN CHAMPION
INBA World ProAm Championships 2nd Place  - Open Women's
Figure Class (Tall Division)

For more information about visit www.lindyolsen.com

# Justine Switalla

*I have been fortunate to have crossed paths with Justine on a couple of occasions, the key stand out being when Justine was presenting the INBA All Female Classic 2012 show in Melbourne and through a mutual friend I was able to spend time with her whilst she was getting ready for the big night. What was really refreshing was to see how real she was – I was welcomed into her home on what would have been a nerve wracking day yet Justine was full of smiles and friendly chats.*

*I next run into Justine at Filex 2013 in Sydney where she spent the weekend between the Oxygen stand and Les Mills Stage where yet again she made the time to say hello and was both warm and welcoming even though she was busy – Justine truly makes time for others.*

*Justine is multitalented, she is a Personal Trainer, Fitness Model, Oxygen Brand Ambassador, BodyScience Sponsored Athlete plus a Les Mills Presenter and here she shares her journey.*

**CJ: How did you first become involved in the sport?**

A decision was made to put all my hard work into practice and show myself what I was made of. I wanted to learn about my body and see what I could achieve when I really set my mind to it.

**CJ: And you work in the Fitness Industry too:**

Yes! I am in many different areas of the industry now. As I have grown and developed over the years and I have wanted to take on new and exciting challenges. I am a Personal Trainer, Les Mills Presenter and instructor for RPM, GRIT and CXWorx, I am a writer, a presenter, an online coach, an author, an Oxygen magazine and Body Science ambassador and a fitness model.

**CJ: Wow that must certainly keep you busy. Do you find that being so involved in the fitness industry complements competing?**

Yes definitely. I have the freedom to train when I want and when competing I can cater my work schedule around my training. Also I am able to make the time to prep and cook my own meals which is essential.

**CJ: So why did you decide to compete?**

Mainly for fun but also as I was keen to get more recognition in the fitness industry.

**CJ: Before you competed, how long had you been training for?**

I was seriously training for around 3 months leading into my first show.

**CJ: And what is it you enjoy most about competing?**

It has been a great stepping stone for me to get exposure within the industry. Also all the amazing likeminded people that it has put me in touch with.

**CJ: Is there anything you don't like about it?**

These days it is very competitive and I see a whole different side to the dangers of serial dieting and over training. I deal with the emotional side of it now by helping girls to get their heads back into normal living and understanding that it isn't healthy to be ripped all year round! Competing does cause a lot of emotional issues for many females and body image issues which is sad!

**CJ: And how far out do you start planning for competition?**

Usually only 6 weeks as I like to maintain a good physique all year round.

**CJ: So this gives you shorter comp prep than most, great. How much does your body fat % and lifestyle change from day to day living when it is competition time?**

I usually sit at 12-14% during the year and to compete I need to be around 9-10%. I measure my progress in the lead up to a show using skin calipers.

**CJ: How does your training routine change in lead up to a show?**

My training is definitely more structured to make sure I hit all muscle groups but it doesn't change that much as it is my diet that changes the most.

**CJ: So what changes do you make with your nutrition in the lead up to a show?**

That too is a lot more structured; I take out all sugars, dairy, starchy carbohydrates and alcohol. I am much more regimented with what I eat and when I eat it. I eat a high protein/high fat diet with minimal carbs during the depletion phase.

**CJ: Can you tell us what typical days eating plan would be during comp prep?**

I have an egg white omelette or chicken with veggies x 4 meals. I only eat chicken so it is very boring just eating chicken for each meal. I will have shakes throughout the day also and have a banana pre weight training session. Once a week I have a treat meal which would be a high carbohydrate meal.

**CJ: And how does this compare to a typical off season day?**

During the off season I have protein smoothie with flaxmeal and supplements for breakfast, then during the day meals consist of omelette with veggies, protein bar, chicken salad, nuts and fruit. Dinner would be chicken or other lean protein with veggies or salad. I like to have a glass of red on the weekends also and a decent treat meal to keep me sane.

**CJ: In terms of exercise now, how often do you train per week and how long is each session generally?**

I exercise 5-6 days per week and my sessions go for no longer than 45mins. I do 3 HIIT sessions a week for cardio and 4 x weight training sessions.

**CJ: What keeps you focused and motivated when you are going through comp prep?**

I find it is easy to stay focused when you have a goal. I like to put my best physique on stage so once I am in the zone it is easy to stay on track.

**CJ: How do you deal with the infamous post competition blues?**

I have competed enough times now that I don't get this. I did get it the first time I competed and it was a process I had to go through alone. It is horrible and I wish I had the support that I give to girls now! With the right support and post comp plan there should be no reason to become depressed or blow out after a show.

**CJ: How do you manage the off season?**

I don't have an off season to be precise. I just live by the 80/20 rule – 80% of the time everything is perfect and 20% for when life pops up with unexpected things. I make sure to live life to the fullest and enjoy the finer things in life as well as keep up my training and good nutrition. It is all about balance, this way you feel in control of your body and do not feel guilty if you do stray from your plan.

**CJ: Can you share your number one Top Tip to anyone either interested in competing or who may currently be in training for a show?**

You have to be committed and you have to be ready to sacrifice a lot of what normal living is. It is a very selfish thing to do as it is hard to be social and have a life outside of eating and the gym. If you can be selfish and stay committed to your goal then you will be fine.

Also not listening to anyone who will try and talk you out of it or put you down in anyway, there will always be people that just don't understand the sport!

**CJ: And what if someone wants to train but not compete what would you advise?**

I would advise them to book in a photoshoot so they can still see their hard work has paid off then if they like what they see they might want to take it further. It is important to have a goal and to see yourself for all the hard work that you put in.

**CJ: Justine has a wealth of competitions under her belt and has excelled in the sport:**

**Competition history**

1st October 2008 Victorian Titles
1st Short class All female classic 2009
1st- Overall best Sports Model All female classic 2009
2nd INBA Australian titles 2009
4th WNBF Asia Pacific titles
3rd Natural Olympia World titles 2009
1st Short class All female classic 2010
1st Overall Sports Model- INBA All female Classic
1st Overall Glamour/Fitness model Nabba NZ 2012

**CJ: Justine can you tell me out of all these shows, what is your biggest highlight or standout memory?**

Definitely the achievement of being a cover girl 3 times! Competing definitely made this possible for me and being a cover girl was a major achievement for me.
Oxygen cover girl August 2010
Fitness Magazine cover girl Nov 2012
Oxygen Workout annual cover girl 2013

**CJ: So what's next for you?**

I have so many things happening in my life over the next 12 months, the biggest one being that I am going to be a mum. I am due to have a baby on Jan 8th 2014 and couldn't be more excited. I am so ready for this next stage of my life and my partner and I are beside ourselves with excitement. I aim to have a healthy pregnancy and then post baby I want to obviously get myself back into tip top shape and prove that if I can do it then all the other mummy's out there can do it too. I will be contributing in the Fit mum's section of Oxygen magazine which I am thrilled about, not only do I get to share my experiences and knowledge with other mum's but have a way to inspire and motivate more women to be the best and most healthy versions of themselves that they can be!

**CJ: A big thank you to Justine for sharing her experiences with us.**

# *Skye Cushway*

Meeting Skye for the first time was a lot of fun. We met in Starbucks during the Sydney Filex Fitness weekend and Skye literally walked off the plane and into the hot seat! Full of energy and smiles, it didn't take long for the two of us to begin chatting like we were old friends. It is this common connection of mutual interests and experience that is just another aspect of the sport that I love.

*Skye began her figure competitor journey in 2010 and achieved outstanding success straight away. Whilst it may look like Skye had only just stepped into the arena, she actually began laying the foundations to develop her physique when she started weight training regularly over 20 years ago. Skye naturally transitioned into the world of health and fitness and has been a PT for over 8 years and it was whilst she was at World Gym in Ashmore that she met her Trainer Jon Davie and then took the plunge to walk out on stage.*

*Here she shares her journey:-*

**CJ: Tell me more about how you got into competing?**

I started with Jon Davie two years before walking out on stage as he was recommended to me by Lindy Olsen who has always been a big inspiration to me – I am now fortunate to be able to call her a friend of mine. I didn't really have any idea what was involved, all

I know was that for so long I had admired girls in the fitness magazines and would say to myself "I want to have a body like that!"

**CJ: Did you know much about competition day and 'show time'?**

I used to watch YouTube videos of the girls in America and had only been to one show before competing.

**CJ: Wow, so your first show experience was actually you competing in it!**

Yes ☺

**CJ: Tell me about this experience:**

Well actually I had gone to compete previously, however I did not have a supportive partner at the time and it was difficult. We split up and I then found the love of my life who was 100% behind me and then when I stepped up to compete at the ANB AsiaPacific Novice Figure in 2010 I won!

**CJ: How did that feel?**

It felt amazing as it was so unexpected, I really couldn't believe it - I thought I was going to be the dud on stage. It did not even enter into my head that I could win - all I was focused on was getting my body into stage shape. I thought a couple of times that it would be good to win, but I wasn't pinning all my hopes and dreams onto winning.

Sometime though you do find that people will blow smoke up your bum and say "you're gonna kill it" yet I didn't really listen to that.

**CJ: After that you began preparing for the INBA All Female Classic in Melbourne**

Yes that was like two weeks after. I went into the open class and as I won that I went through to the overalls. That was a big line up and I thought there is no chance in hell that I'm going to win this and when they called my name I couldn't believe it.

**CJ: Can you remember that feeling?**

Yes it was the best feeling in the world! Ohmygod I was screaming inside to myself and I started to cry. It's hard to describe how amazing the feeling was – it truly was the best feeling in the world.

**CJ: And after the show, what happened?**

After the All Female I got selected to go to Vegas and I came 7th out 50 something girls so I was happy with that.

**CJ: That's amazing, what a phenomenal year for you.**

Yes it was but when you are new to the sport and win and then you don't win it is hard, it was a big dent in the ego – not that I am up myself, it's just that when you get used to winning you expect to win so it was a great lesson to learn early on. I hadn't put 100% into preparing for that show, I cheated more than normal and as everyone was telling me I looked great, I thought yeah I'll be alright. Whilst it was challenging it was also good to realise that there will be girls out there who will diet a bit harder or spend more time practicing posing.

**CJ: So what was the deciding factor for you to say yes I'm going to compete?**

I think my life all of a sudden clicked together, there wasn't one deciding factor. I found a supportive partner and I had been talking

24

about it for years, I'm a doer not a talker so I decided I am going to do this now, contacted Jon and said yes I am ready to go.

*It was during 2010 that Skye was approached by Musashi and is now a sponsored athlete.*
I couldn't believe this too when this happened, I was so blown away, and still am 3 years later. I can't thank them enough for all their support.

*Skye then competed in 2011 and 2012 with IFBB, she competed in FitX in Melbourne and has placed 2nd and 3rd in Open Figure.*

**CJ: How did you manage comp prep with working full time as a PT?**

Well I didn't find that it was that hard. I had seen others go through the process and they would say how horrible they felt and I was waiting to feel crap yet I felt amazing through it. Yes the last week was hard but as I work with someone who cares about health first it was easier. I did not restrict any specific macronutrient group and I did not do endless hours of cardio.

**CJ: So how was your progress managed?**

Each week tweaks were made slightly to food and increased the cardio towards the end depending on how my body fat was coming down.

**CJ: What do you not like about the sport?**

I find it more and more now that girls are damaging their bodies unnecessarily as they strive to win and chase the dream of being a pro. Unfortunately many girls are doing things to themselves that are unhealthy and beautiful girls are now changing their look as they are being driven by their ego to step over anyone and do whatever they can to get the trophy and pro card which is sad as you don't get paid for it – that's why you compete for the love of the sport.

**CJ:  So how do you keep it real?**

I have a beautiful family; this definitely plays a lot in it.  I have a gorgeous man and I am family focused – I have my priorities set. Winning is not everything to me, I enjoy competing and I do it to also help promote my business as this helps Clients know that I can help them go through the same experiences, whether or not they are competing.  Most of my clients have everyday general goals who have been with me for years.

**CJ:  How far out from a show do you start preparing?**

I normally start about 20 weeks out and that is just focusing on eating clean and tracking progress every 4 weeks until it gets to 12 weeks out.  Then after that I see Jon weekly and he monitors progress weekly through skin fold measurements.  We go on how I look rather than weight on the scale and I try not to weigh myself generally as it can do your head in if the numbers are not going down.  It's like playing mind games with yourself.

**CJ:  Yes it is – I have a wardrobe of different size clothes – off season, comp prep and competition ready.  This can also play with your mind when you find yourself going from smaller sizes to the normal ones!**

Yes I know I tried my jeans on and they are a size 10 yet there was a voice that said, uh they're not that baggy anymore!

**CJ: Ha I know, it is important to remember that this is normal and most of us go through the same headspace and it's important to recognise that it's ok to be back in normal sizes and not to be obsessive!**

Yes it's great we can talk openly about it and laugh.

**CJ: What do you enjoy most about competing?**

I really enjoy the feeling of waking up on competition day – it feels like Christmas to see your body in its ripped state, seeing your abs and seeing the result of your hard work and dedication. It's such a great sense of achievement and I feel so proud of myself, it blows my mind.

I also like having a goal, the control of staying focused and committed to an end result. I feel when I am competing I feel great, even if people around me are saying oh why are you doing that.

**CJ: Is there anything you don't like about the sport?**

Yes I really don't like the diva attitude; I have had a few bad experiences that I let get to me, especially when I went to Vegas with one particular girl who made it very uncomfortable.

I also don't like everyone's perception that it's bad for you to compete. If you do it naturally and smartly then you don't mess your body up. A lot of people go crashing into a show and pick a show as a weight loss goal and go head strong into it when the goal is unrealistic and this is what causes a massive rebound. This is when it is bad for your health.

**CJ: How do you deal with post competition blues?**

At first it was hard, I didn't know what to do, I just went crazy and ate crazy like everyone does and of course I gained too much body fat which made me feel crap about myself. It was hard as people would look at you like, oh you are not this little thing anymore.

I do not think there is enough education about what happens to you mentally after you no longer have such a huge focus.

**CJ: Yes you are right and sadly too often people think that they can maintain the body that they showed on stage – again this is unrealistic as you have had to restrict yourself to get there and it is unhealthy mentally to keep living in a restricted mindset – this is what causes the rebound binges.**

**CJ: So how does your lifestyle change during the lead up to a show?**

It doesn't change that much to be honest, obviously I reduce the amount of social functions I attend – not that I'm that social – and of course the weekend treats are removed. I will still go out for dinner maybe every couple of weeks and I ensure that food is cooked to my requirements.

From a weight perspective, I try to stay within 5 to 6 kgs of competition weight, rather than focus on body fat%. It is easy to get hung up on these figures and again it does mess with your head. It took me a long time to let this go.

**CJ: Well when you are up on stage it is all about how you look – the judges are not asking for your weight or body fat % so it is important to focus on clean eating and smart training off season so you get the developments you are after.**
**What about training – how does that change in comp prep?**

Off season I would do 5 sessions a week, split routine, changing it every 6 weeks. I do a lot of compound movements to maintain muscle mass. Leading up to a show I would do 6 sessions – I would do 2 leg sessions and from 10 weeks out I move to all over body workouts at a high intensity. I will also do 45 mins cardio a day as well until the last 4 weeks out where I will do 2 cardio sessions – only ever low intensity walking.

**CJ: How about nutrition – how does this change between normal and comp prep?**

Well I am actually gluten and dairy intolerant and have not eaten these for the last couple years – at first I thought ohmygod how will I live without oats! My body functions better without dairy and gluten, yet for most of my clients this type of meal plan would not be suitable. Currently my routine now looks like this:

Morning Cardio
Breakfast – sweet potato with fish/chicken and veges
Snack – capsicum and turkey or beans with coconut oil
Snack – capsicum and turkey or beans with coconut oil plus fruit before weights
Weights Session
Post workout- sweet potato (or pumpkin) with fish/chicken and veges
Snack – capsicum and turkey
In the evening I will have almond meal and egg whites and will often mix this up with mixed nuts or seeds also have nuts and seeds and at the end of the day have almond meal with egg whites.

Protein sources are normally fish or chicken and I occasionally eat red meat – although in my younger days I was a vegetarian!

In the lead up to a show I will adjust portion sizes and reduce where necessary the closer it gets to show day and I intuitively listen to what my body likes and is asking for.

**CJ: Do you take any supplements around training?**

Try not to rely on pre workouts however I do use the amino range of Musashi products. Generally I try to have protein shakes only after training.

**CJ: How do you stay focused/motivated when competing?**

Of course Oxygen magazine keeps me motivated and I like looking at pictures. I have a vision board with my goals on which helps and a few of these have come true already.

**CJ: And do you have any idols that you follow to help stay motivated?**

Lindy Olsen is someone I really admire – not only within the sport but also out of it too as she keeps it real and I feel really comfortable with her. I am so thankful she is how I thought she would be. I look up to Janet Kane as well, she is a beautiful person, Anne Marie is a good friend of mine who competes with the IFBB. In terms of the American girls I look to would be Pauline Nordin – she is awesome as there is no BS and she is so successful with what she created from just a blog plus I met Ava Cowan I really like – I met her at FitX.

**CJ: How do you manage the off season and post competition binging?**

Book a photoshoot for couple of weeks after the show and keep setting goals that excite you. I learnt my mistakes early on and ate too much after first shows, I was even eating foods that I normally wouldn't  as I got it into my head that I had finished now so I could relax. I had no goals to help keep me on track.

Now I slowly start introducing small treats at the weekend and focus on eating clean the majority of the time and this is how I manage the off season too. I find that I eat clean all week, sometimes have a mid-week pick me up treat and then Friday or Saturday night will have dinner out or a takeaway.

**CJ: Skye, can you share your number one Top Tip to anyone either interested in competing or currently in training for a show?**

Keep it real – do it for yourself and don't compare yourself to others. Stay off of social media and try not to dwell on the negative things. If you tell everyone you are tired of course you will feel tired plus remember that no one is holding a gun to you head making you compete so just enjoy the journey, this is what it's all about, you will learn a lot about yourself and your body.

**CJ: If someone wants to train but not compete what would you advise?**

Do a photoshoot if you don't want to compete and work at getting your body in the best shape of your life. Set yourself a goal and work towards it. Then be realistic about what is achievable for you.

**CJ: Can you share you biggest highlight or standout memory from your competition career?**

Winning the overall at All Female Classic in 2010, being on the cover of Oxygen Magazine twice as well as meeting so many beautiful people in this industry.

**CJ: So what is next for you Skye?**

I am returning to the stage in October 2013 to compete in the ANB and INBA Shows. I tried IFBB for two years and it's just not for me, I am definitely suited to the natural federations and can't wait to get back up on stage later this year.

**CJ: Thank you so much for sharing your journey, experiences and pearls of wisdom! Any final words?**

I love teaching woman how they can have their dream body without going to extremes. I'm based on the Gold Coast and I train one on one or via online training programs so contact me on 0415 385 101 or email me on vanillaskye23@hotmail.com.

# *Lesley Maxwell*

*Lesley has created her own league and has truly redefined what it means to be over 50 and feeling fabulous. Lesley is a mother of three and has more than 20 body sculpting titles to her name. The highlight was representing Australia in New York where she won the prestigious Miss USA Figure Championship.*

*Here Lesley shows us that 'age is no barrier' and being over 50 means you can do whatever you set your mind to!*

**CJ: Lesley, can you share your background and how you become involved in competing?**

I have always led a healthy lifestyle and have been fascinated with how diet and exercise can affect your health and the shape of your body. I have worked as a PT for over ten years and have a life-long passion for health and fitness. Competing takes this to a whole new level! What first got me inspired was seeing a documentary on television about competing with these glamorous hard bodied women on stage who looked gorgeous. I thought I'd like to do that and so I set my mind to it. One of the girls was actually Lindy Olsen!

**CJ: How long ago was this?**

My first competition was in 2005. I located the gym in Melbourne (MBS) where Lindy Olsen was training and I went to meet her as I was so enthused. There were fit bodies everywhere and a feeling of excitement took hold of me. I knew straight away that this was something that I wanted to do!

**CJ: So was this why you decided to compete?**

I've always loved feeling fit and healthy and looking after my body but the thought of pushing myself even further really appealed to me. I wanted a challenge which would take me over my limits both physically and mentally and body sculpting was the answer

**CJ: So let's talk about your first show, how far out did you start planning for it?**

I did four months of competition preparation which was fairly intense. This included weight training, competition dieting and posing practice, I picked a show, set a date and it was all go from there. My first competition was the WFF/NABBA in Victoria and I was in Figure Masters 35+.

**CJ: Do you remember how your first show felt?**

It was an exciting day and I felt really ready to compete. Back stage was quite an experience as everyone was being tanned and there were semi naked bodies everywhere. You could hear the audience applause as the music belted out as competitors were performing their routines.

All of a sudden it was my event my turn to strut my stuff! Before I knew it there I was in front of a crowd wearing a teeny tiny bikini and a pair of stilettoes. My thoughts were "What had I done and could I really do this"? I took a deep breath and away I went. All went smoothly and I still remember the thrill when the MC called my name for first place, I was so surprised that I had won I nearly fell off the stage!

After this I competed in the Nationals in Queensland which was about 3 weeks later and I won second place. Then, although I still trained as it is part of my life I took a break from competing for a couple of years.

It was funny I only ever wanted to tick the box and do one competition, yet in 2008 I thought that's it! I want to do more. I have now done a total of 27 individual competitions!

**CJ: That's phenomenal!**

I just love it, I enjoy getting my body in tip top shape and feeling great. Some of the shows I was able to compete in more than one category so this helped notch up the number of titles I won. For instance I often competed in Open plus the Masters and then into the Overall.

**CJ: You certainly sound like you love the sport – what do you enjoy most about it?**

Apart from the feeling of being in the best shape it is definitely the camaraderie with the other girls. You have all been on an incredible journey together and have broken through personal barriers, shared food, travelled, trained, laughed and cried together. It's this understanding of what each other has gone through that creates great friendships.

**CJ: Anything you don't like?**

Hmm there is nothing I don't like really – oh maybe removing the dream tan afterwards!

**CJ: Ha I actually hate putting it on too! How do you prepare for a show?**

Well I am never far out of competition shape and I stay within 3kg of my stage weight. I have always been interested in the nutritional aspect of food and focus on working towards macronutrient goals rather than count calories. I have learnt that I would rather 'eat' my way into a show than starve. I focus on exercise and aim to maintain food intake as close to normal as possible. I also want to make it as easy as possible by maintaining a good physique all year round.

**CJ: You are obviously in great shape, do you find this hard to maintain at all?**

No not at all, I believe in optimal nutrition to nourish my body regardless of whether I'm competing or not. I make sure I eat the right foods and never go hungry. I do not eat wheat, sugar or processed foods.

If everyone understood the benefits of eating clean and how easy it can be they would be surprised at how good they would feel. Their body will respond in such a positive way regardless of age. So many people seem to battle with their weight and when I work with my clients I enjoy showing them how to make it easier to get great results.

**CJ: Can you share your nutrition and training regime?**

Well I believe that the ratio of macronutrients I consume is vitally important, I focus on ensuring I get enough protein and essential fatty acids in my diet. I weight train 4 times a week with a split routine which I frequently change every two weeks. Off season I still weight train four times weekly and never miss a session as I like to maintain lean body tissue (muscle).

I normally walk 3 to 5 times a week off season as I find it relaxing. During comp prep I will increase the number of walks to sometimes twice daily and add some interval training too. I always have one complete day off a week from exercise.

**CJ: What keeps you focused and motivated when getting ready for a show?**

Well it's the thought of getting my body in the best shape possible. I truly love pushing my body to the limits, this keeps me motivated. Every week I am consistent with my lifestyle so when it comes to preparing for a show I already have the habits set. It would be terrible for me if I couldn't train for some reason, for me this would feel like a punishment. Being on stage is such a thrill and when all the hard work is done you can really enjoy yourself on the day!

**CJ:  And how do you track your progress?**

I know what the nutrient values are in food and I am able to monitor this through the day. I never keep a food diary, weigh my food or keep a training log. I am so in tune with my body, I have a good feeling of where I am at and what I need to do.

Consistency is the key with your training and clean eating. If you maintain a good off season physique then you can monitor visual changes easily making it easier to get back on stage.

**CJ:  Who are you idols?**

I really admire women who maintain a healthy lifestyle after competing and spread the word on health and fitness. You need determination and confidence in yourself to compete. I believe that every single competitor represents about one hundred who didn't make it to the stage. It's a special sisterhood you share with your fellow competitors so there are so many I admire.

Lindy Olsen is a wonderful example of living the fitness lifestyle. Lindy has inspired so many women and has also done so much for the fitness industry.

**CJ: Is there one standout memory from all your shows?**

My favourite memory was definitely the worlds in New York where I won the US Figure Open category. I was on stage with girls of all ages as I believe this sport is about bodyshape rather than age! It was amazing, I had a successful comp season and this was my 10th competition in twelve weeks. My body responded well and I was completely focused.

**CJ: What is your number one Top Tip to anyone either interested in competing or currently in training for a show?**

Be honest with yourself and stay consistent with your clean eating. Learn to listen to your body and nourish it with food it needs to build muscle rather than eating for taste or pleasure alone. As good food can taste great too!

Competing really is a fantastic goal to ensure you stay focused and don't go off track with your training and clean eating.

Stay focused and believe in yourself.

**CJ: What if someone wants to train but not compete what would you advise?**

Although health and fitness is a lifestyle and not a hobby it's a good idea to set a goal to begin. Maybe even a photoshoot or a special occasion to work towards. When you reach your goal maintaining your new body will become easier if you are aware of what you are eating and exercise effectively. Our bodies really do respond well to clean eating and never fails to amaze me how you can change the shape of your body through diet and exercise.

**CJ: And what does the future hold for you? Will you compete again?**

Competing has opened many doors for me. I love being involved in the fitness industry. It's wonderful to feel that you may have made a positive difference to someone's life.

I am delighted to say that I have been an Oxygen Covergirl and am now a regular contributor for Oxygen too. Also I have written a book 'Get the Body You Want' plus started 'Oui Fitness' which is an on line training website and keeps me pretty busy. I haven't hung my competition shoes up yet and am actually thinking of competing at the end of this year.

I can be contacted at www.ouifitness.com.au and would love to hear from you.

# *Katrin Hapala*

*Katrin, or Trin as she is known as to her nearest and dearest has a very unique and different experience with competing than others in this book. Katrin does not work within the health or fitness world, in fact she is an executive assistant in the corporate world and is a mother of 2 young children! If this didn't keep her busy enough she also runs a personal training business.*

*I consider myself to be extremely fortunate to know Katrin on a personal level and call her a friend of mine. We first met at a workshop on competing and stayed in touch ever since. This is a true testament of how amazing this sport can be and so many other competitors have formed lifelong friendships in this way too. The support and understanding you have of each other's journey certainly deepens the friendship.*

*Trin (as I like to call her) met at our favourite local health food shop for lunch and a catch up. Here she gives her insights into competing from a different perspective.*

**CJ: Trin, can you share with us your background as well as how long have you been sports modeling/competing for?**

I am a 32 year old mother of 2 young children, originally born in the Czech Republic, my family emigrated when I was 3 years old to Australia. I started training and exercising seriously in the gym when I was about 17. It was a mixture of weights and aerobics and I was definitely a cardio queen with a passion for high energy and high impact aerobics! I would see all the fit looking girls in the gym and found them very inspiring.

I started preparing for my first show in 2010, 9 months after having my first child. I decided to set a big goal that would challenge me as well as assist in being in great shape post pregnancy.

Then, in 2010 I competed in a total of 7 shows! After that I took some time off to have my second child and I plan to compete again in either 2014 or 2015.

**CJ: And how did you first become involved in competing?**

I have always had a keen interest in the sport. In the back of my mind I knew that one day I would compete. It was in late December 2009 when I started to write down my goals for 2010 that it was decided that 2010 would be the year I would pursue my goal of competing. This was when the dream became a reality.

**CJ: Why did you decide to compete?**

I decided to compete as I had always wanted to see how my body would change through diet and training. It is also a goal that I wanted to accomplish. I believe that the knowledge that I have gained through competing has given me a better understanding of how to live a healthy well balanced life. I have learned to understand how my body responds to certain foods at certain times of the day and different types of training. I have become more aware of my body and how it responds to nutrition and training.

**CJ: So why 2010?**

I guess I was looking for a big goal to pursue and this was a major goal I have always had. I had always said that it was something I wanted to do and I was fortunate that my partner was very supportive of this dream and encouraged me to pursue it. Support is such a big thing!

**CJ: How long had you been training for prior to making this decision?**

I played netball in my primary school years and went onto playing representative netball in my high school years. I was also a member of my local surf club at the time and competed at a national level. At about the age of 17 I joined the local gym and have been a gym member ever since. You could say that I have always done some sort of training. I have always been a keen soft sand runner.

At the gym I loved participating in aerobic classes and weight training yet I didn't understand the principles of weight training – every session would be full body, there was no structure to reps, set or rest! It was always the same workout each time!

**CJ: So where did you go to learn more and increase your knowledge?**

Well I had never been to a show before and went into competing a little blind! I did a lot of research online, reading as well as speaking to others that had competed.

**CJ: Many other competitors work within the fitness industry and are able to learn from others around them, you are not involved this way were you?**

I have just recently started up my own personal training business called Muscle Mechanic where I train clients from my studio in South Cronulla as well as running outdoor group training.

Before this I have always worked within the corporate world, ever since leaving high school at 17! Yet always outside of work my passion has been for health and fitness.

**CJ: And now you have a wealth of experience and knowledge!**

Yes, the knowledge that I have gained from competing has been invaluable. I believe that working in the fitness industry and competing do complement each other. The same principles apply eat, train and rest.

**CJ: Did you get a Trainer to help you with your competition prep for 2010?**

I had always completed research online and I chose to go with an online trainer.

**CJ: How did this work?**

The process for this was email 'check-ins' every fortnight with photos of front and back plus my weight as well as how I was feeling. After this, there would be diet or training modifications made depending on my progress. I also learnt to pose with my trainer and had one to one posing sessions each week in the lead up to each show. I have had two routines choreographed, one by my then trainer and the other by Jo Rogers from Style on Stage.

**CJ: How did you manage practicing posing with being a mum to a young baby?**

(Trin laughs) I had to do it at night after everyone had gone to bed!

**CJ: Wow that's dedication!**

It was funny, in the same week I decided to compete I also returned to work from maternity leave, and brought a trainer on board! It was quite a challenge at first, yet it was like anything once you get into a routine you manage to fit it all in. You have to prioritise – obviously there were a few ups and downs in the lead up to the show, especially when I had to do daily cardio! Luckily my partner made all my meals for me whilst I was out walking and this was also when the baby was sleeping – hence everything was done late at night when it was possible.

I was also breastfeeding and found this challenging; I had already planned to stop breast feeding before the first show as I knew in the lead up this would no longer be possible so again it was all about preparation. I was concerned about supplements and made sure I was not taking these around feeding times.

I did also find that I got tired a lot, but you just push on through!

**CJ: So you had the date in mind for your first competition, how long out did you start preparing for this?**

For me it was a little different when I was competing. The first time I started preparing was in January for a May competition. The focus was on my diet and then when it came to 12 weeks out of the show I wasn't struggling or feeling depleted. It was the long prep that helped make dieting easier and more enjoyable.

If I was to prepare for a competition now I would say I would need 10-12 weeks. All depends on my body fat percentage at the time of deciding to compete.

**CJ: How much does your body fat percentage change and life style, from day to day living to competition time?**

I generally live a healthy and clean lifestyle so my life doesn't change very much in relation to food. My training in non-competition time is very relaxed and not as structured as it would be during competition time.

**CJ: How do you measure your progress in the lead up to a show?**

My progress was measured by my body weight and front and back photographs.

**CJ: How does your training routine change in lead up to a show?**

Training becomes very strict and structured with cardio and weight training sessions.

**CJ: How often would you exercise each week, and how long is each session generally?**

If preparing for a show cardio would be 40-60mins and weight training about 40mins 6 times a week. My training now is mainly weight training 40mins 3 times a week with 1 x 30min HIIT session and 1 x 60-90min power yoga in a heated room. Off season the focus is on muscle growth whilst in the last few weeks of comp prep cardio increases and weight training changes to full body workouts with very high reps – like 75-100!

**CJ: What about nutrition? What changes are made in the lead up to a show?**

Leading up to a show the main changes with nutrition revolve around reducing portion sizes  and eating more frequently. My carbohydrate to protein ratios also change.

**CJ: Can you describe a typical day eating plan during comp prep?**

Meal 1 – Oats and egg whites
Meal 2 – protein shake
Meal 3 – chicken, sweet potato and greens
Meal 4 – fish and greens
Meal 5 – chicken and greens

## CJ: How does this compare to a typical day eating off season?

Meal 1 – Organic oats, egg whites and coffee
Meal 2 – Almonds and apple
Meal 3 – Chicken or steak with veggies, a hardboiled egg and either rice or sweet potato
Meal 4 – Banana and protein shake
Meal 5 – Each night it varies but usually some sort of protein, salmon/barramundi, lentils, tofu or steak with rice or sweet potato and veggies or salad.

Off season I eat more carbs such as brown rice, sweet potato and fruit plus increase portion sizes and have treats on the weekend.

I love the off season as this is the time to enjoy good food and training that delivers results.

## CJ: How do you stay focused and motivated when competing?

Having that passion to succeed and achieve that goal that I have set myself. It isn't for anyone else but for me. I want my children to see me as a positive role model who has determination. I want them to see that you can accomplish your dreams and that if you set a goal, follow through with it.

## CJ: Let's talk more now about your first show

That was amazing, I remember being extremely nervous – I am normally shy in front of a large group of people so for me to walk out on stage in a tiny bikini was nerve wracking! Once I walked off that stage I wanted to go straight back on and it was since then that I became hooked!

I placed 3rd in my first show, Novice Figure and after this competed two weeks later and again placed 3rd.

**CJ: After these two shows you competed in the ANB Asia Pacific – how did this feel?**

I remember thinking that I was glad I competed in this show. It was a huge eye opener and made me want to compete more. I wanted to succeed, the girls on stage were amazing and it showed what hard work and determination can do.

**CJ: And your first win came at the ANB Central Coast show?**

Yes it was amazing, such an overwhelming feeling. I had my family there too and it was a surreal feeling. I won the short figure, novice figure and the overall! After this I competed at the INBA NSW show and this is probably my favourite show as I felt that I looked the best at this one in terms of physique, mindset and experience.

**CJ: When you won the overall at the INBA what was going through your mind? How did that feel?**

You stop and think are they calling my number?! You do a little check side to side and you don't want to step out in case you have it wrong yet you are the last one standing there without a trophy. It is such a great feeling, you can't stop smiling, all that hard work has paid off!

**CJ: Would there be any post show treat?**

Ohmygoodness – yes, normally the treat would be a pizza! I would go straight to Crust and get a pizza in my tan, hair and bling! After the third show they got used to me and sometimes I was seeing other competitors there too!

**CJ: Then it was off to the Nationals, tell me more about this?**

That show was a lot of fun, the level of competition was outstanding and to be on that stage with those at that level was incredible, yet I was also sad as I knew the season was coming to an end and this was my last show.

There was actually one more show after this, the IFBB show which I did for fun and also to gain more experience. I had such a great year and I wanted to get as many shows under my belt as possible as I did not know when I would be competing again as we were hoping to extend our family.

**CJ: Can you share what you enjoy most about competing?**

The biggest thing I enjoy about competing is the discipline and the challenge. Learning about my body and how it responds to training and nutrition. I love the challenge of dieting, it's not easy yet it is so rewarding resisting temptation to achieve a goal. I did enjoy it and obviously there were some low points. When these occurred, I remembered the reason why I was dieting. Plus, seeing my body change in a positive way helped stay on track with the diet.

**CJ: What is your number one Top Tip to anyone either interested in competing or currently in training for a show?**

Stay consistent and persistent. Seek the help from a good trainer and only listen to them, not anyone else. Too many people have an opinion and too many interjections can cause confusion for someone new to this sport.

**CJ: What if someone wants to train but not compete what would you advise?**

Set yourself some goals, get the help of either a fitness professional or a friend that knows what they are doing.

**Competition history**

- 2010 ANB South Coast Championships – 3rd novice figure

- 2010 ANB Sydney Championships – 3rd novice figure / 3rd short figure
- 2010 ANB Asia Pacific Championships – 4th short figure
- 2010 ANB Central Coast – 1st short figure/1st novice figure/overall women's champion
- 2010 INBA NSW Titles – 1st short figure/overall women's champion
- 2010 ANB National Titles – 2nd short figure
- 2010 IFBB NSW and Australian Titles – 1st NSW short figure

**CJ: From all of your shows, what is the highlight?**

For me, every show that I have competed in is a standout memory. I enjoy meeting all the likeminded people and the different experiences each show brings.

The ANB Asia Pacific in the finals, standing next to the more experienced girls was amazing and the genuine-ness in their smiles when they congratulated me.

**CJ: Any embarrassing moments at all back stage?**

I don't think so, when you are in that environment everyone is practically naked anyway and we are all in the same boat. I am lucky enough to have never had any bad backstage experiences and everyone has always been friendly and helpful towards each other. This is what I love about the sport, everyone is so supportive of each other, even though they are competing against you. You are all there for the same reason, everyone has put in their 100% effort.

When you are backstage on comp day you do have to focus on getting ready to get up there and shine and if there is any negativity around you just avoid it.

**CJ: How do you deal with post competition blues?**

I am always prepared with a plan that is written down. The plan tells me what I am going to do the next day. This lists my food and activity. In the back of my mind I have already set myself the next goal whether it is another show or enrolling in a course.

I did feel empty for a little while after my last show yet I just kept going, you have to, you still train every day and my meals were still made. It was more relaxed generally, I got time to relax with my family and spend more time with them.

**CJ: Do you have any role models?**

I don't have a particular role model as there are so many influential people around me. I admire anyone who is dedicated, passionate, hardworking and self-motivated. This applies to people in health and fitness and successful business men and women.

**CJ: Is there anything you don't like about competing?**

Negative responses from those who are uneducated about the sport. There is a negative perception from many and being asked if I take steroids is upsetting, especially as I am 100% natural and a mother. People don't understand why we do certain things we do in the sport which help us get stage ready.

**CJ: Well thank you for your honesty and showing us that anyone can get up and give competing a go! I can't wait to see you back on stage soon!**

Katrin Hapala is a qualified personal trainer, an executive assistant, figure competitor and mother of two young children. Katrin has a passion for helping others with their health and fitness goals and specialises in one on one female personal training and outdoor training. She can be contacted at trainer@musclemechanic.com.au or through her website www.musclemechanic.com.au.

# *Amanda Steer*

*My first encounter with Amanda was watching her accompany Lindy in the states on her 2010 journey to compete in the world titles following the video blog that was created by Dallas, Lindy and Amanda. I found her to be so much fun, full of energy and definitely had a zest for life and truly painted the portrait of keeping it real!*

*Amanda is certainly down to earth and combines her passion for competing and healthy living with a full time role in the police force. Here she gives her unique perspective.*

**CJ: How long have you been sports competing for?**

I started in 2009.

**CJ: How did you first become involved in the sport?**

I became an RPM instructor and I really wanted to increase my fitness and 'look the part'. I wanted to be able to have a physique that would somewhat inspire class participants to reach their own health and fitness goals. Initially it was about that and cleaning up my diet, fellow instructor Joely Davie introduced me to her husband who helped me with this which then turned into the idea of competing.

**CJ: And you don't work in the fitness industry full time do you?**

No, I am a full time Police officer so my employment in the fitness industry as such is minimal and I instruct 2 RPM classes per week.

**CJ: Do you find that being involved in the fitness industry complements competing?**

In relation to my RPM classes impacting on competing I simply just needed to take a couple of weeks off before shows.

**CJ: How long had you been training for before competing?**

I have always trained since I was old enough to set foot in a gym! Specifically to compete I started to train in 2008.

**CJ: What do you enjoy most about competing?**

The journey it takes me to get on stage.  And getting my nails done!

**CJ: And is there anything you don't like about it?**

I don't like the tan! I struggle in heels a little too!

**CJ: How far out do you start planning for competition?**

I work through a 20 week preparation with my coach.  Slow and steady I think makes things a little easier and is definitely healthier for me.  I do 4 weight sessions a week in my off season with the focus on always trying to make little improvements.

**CJ: How much does your body fat percentage and lifestyle change from day to day living to competition time?**

I don't like to let myself go as such too much.  I want to try and inspire people all year round.  To be honest most don't find the look on stage aesthetically pleasing. I am about 5 or 6 kg heavier than my stage weight in the off season. As far as lifestyle changes go. I stop road riding probably about 3 months out from shows and I stop surfing about 6 weeks out. I definitely miss surfing but I find I generally don't have the time or energy. One of my biggest struggles in prep is doing shift work. I find that it fatigues me pretty easily as the shows get closer.

**CJ: How do you measure your progress in the lead up to a show?**

I follow the scales closely and get skin folds done regularly to monitor how I am coming in. I also get skinfolds done about once a month in my off season which helps to ensure I am not putting on too much weight.

**CJ: How does your training routine change in lead up to a show?**

Mainly it is the cardio that slowly gets increased. During the off season, I do 4 weight sessions a week and cardio most days, for no longer than 45mins. Unless of course I am on my road bike and that could be up to 3 hrs! I like mixing things up off season.

**CJ: How does your nutrition change in lead up to a show?**

My meals increase; I have more vegetables and ensure I have protein in every meal.

**CJ: How do you stay focused and motivated when competing?**

I don't struggle a great deal with this. It's almost like a switch gets flicked and I just get on with the job at hand.

**CJ: How do you deal with post competition blues?**

I have been fortunate that I haven't suffered a great deal from this. There are other things I enjoy doing so I usually enjoy getting back into riding and surfing. We all allow ourselves treats after competing so I make the most of the extra energy I have and maximise my weight training sessions. I am a pretty happy person so I usually just enjoy this and the extra time I have on my hands!

**CJ: So how do you manage the off season?**

I love my off season. I eat reasonably well. I get at least 5 meals in a day. If I want to I will have treats moderately and generally don't have to go without anything. I enjoy surfing and road riding too.

**CJ: Describe a typical day eating during the off season?**

I have a minimum of 5 meals a day. I am a bit of a dairy cow so there are usually 3 serves of dairy a day. I have a love affair with a good coffee and only started drinking it when I was 31 (yes finally a grown up!) I love a good skinny flat white. Protein in every meal, 3 vegetable serves a day, good carbs and fats.

**CJ: So what is your number one Top Tip to anyone either interested in competing or currently in training for a show?**

Either do it 100% or don't bother. Blunt yes, but I don't believe it is something you can go into half heartedly.

**CJ: What if someone wants to train but not compete what would you advise?**

Go right ahead but I certainly wouldn't advise them to try and become stage lean. It is not realistically maintainable or healthy to try and maintain such low levels of body fat. Plus without the compelling goal of getting on stage you won't do what you need to do to achieve it.

## Competition history

2009 ANB Asia Pacific Novice 1st place
2010 INBA Open class 3rd place
2010 Asia Pacific Open class 2nd place
2011 ANB Nationals Open class 1st place

**CJ: And what is your standout memory?**

Winning my first show, you know actually getting myself up on stage. I found my first prep to be the toughest.

**CJ: Thank You!**

# Sian Toal WBFF PRO

*I have known Sian for many years now, first meeting in London when we both were teaching group exercise classes at the same gym. I feel incredibly proud of Sian as I have seen her full journey. From taking the first step on stage, to building a successful PT business with her partner, to providing support and inspiration to so many, I have seen it all so when she was awarded her pro card in 2013 I was ecstatically happy for her.*

*Sian is here not only to represent the British but also to provide her incredible journey with us.*

**CJ:  Sian, when did you first start to compete?**

I have been a competing physique athlete since 2011 and recently turned Pro in April 2013 with the WBFF.  Up to that point, I had a dream to compete and be a fitness model, I loved the look of the cover girls on magazines like, 'Oxygen' yet never pursued it.

**CJ:  So had you always been active?**

Up until 2011 I'd only ever trained for a sport or as a dancer.  I was also a Group Fitness Instructor so how my body looked was just a by product of my job and the events I was training for.  However, I have always had involvement in some kind of sport or physical activity, growing up in a large family with PE Teachers for Parents definitely helped!

**CJ: We met as we both worked in the fitness industry, can you tell me more about your background and what you do now?**

I began training to become a Personal Trainer a year after graduation from a Performing Arts Degree, when I found inspiration from a Dance Fitness Trainer and discovered a passion for Nutrition.

I went on to become a successful Personal Trainer and Studio Instructor working within Gyms and Health Clubs.

I now run Onpoint Training, a private Personal Training studio near Liverpool Street in London with my fiancé Jay Benedetti. I also privately train clients in their homes in Notting Hill and recently accompanied one of my clients whilst she filmed the BBC TV Show, 'Dragons Den'. This was true training on location!

I specialise in Body Transformations and use weight training systems to achieve results. Through Onpoint, Jay and I are starting to create our exclusive 'train abroad' program plus I have had the opportunity to write for magazines such as 'Workout Magazine', 'Bodyfit Magazine', 'WBFF Fitness and Fashion' and 'The Huffington Post'.

**CJ: Do you find working within fitness complements competing?**

Being a trainer and competitor has taught me discipline, focus and given me the ability to plan and see out goals. I have learnt a great deal about myself and found my strengths through the process. There are obvious benefits to having your own place to train! But I have a natural desire to learn and being surrounded by other trainers and a great coach has helped me grow as a trainer and competitor.

**CJ: So why did you decide to compete?**

A huge factor in deciding to compete was to find my confidence again. I have been a performer most of my life, but in my 2nd year at University I suffered a severe confidence crisis and went through quite a low period. Things got better over time and I found confidence again in my work and teaching group fitness, but the last thing on my list was to get back on stage as a performer. Competing brought it all together for me, learning to commit to a goal, plan and prepare, focus mentally and physically and then putting it up there on stage.

My fiancé, Jay, also inspired me. I went to watch him compete and he encouraged me to follow my dream and has supported me all the way through to earning Pro Status.

**CJ: How long had you been training for before you got into competing?**

I have danced since the age of three, leading up to undertaking a BA Performing Arts Degree at Middlesex University. I also trained as a sprinter at Loughborough University as a teenager. So training was already part of my life.

In terms of training in the gym with the emphasis on trying to improve my physique, this has been since 2004.

**CJ: All the dancing and sprinting is what gives you such incredible leg conditioning which I have been envious of for years! Sian, what do you enjoy most about competing?**

You meet many fascinating and inspirational characters when competing and form such great friendships. I also love to train and see what I can push my body to achieve. I'm always learning in this industry and I like to develop try new things.

Of course I love the end result when all the gloss is put on top of the finished product and I know I've worked hard, been consistent, had the ups and downs, pain and glory and at the end point it all feels worth it.

**CJ: Is there anything you don't like about it?**

It can be quite a small world and everyone likes a good gossip!

**CJ:  How far out do you start planning for competition?**

I'll be following a comp diet 16 weeks out, spending the first 4 weeks getting into the flow of cleaning things up a bit, eating regularly and preparing food in advance for the week.

**CJ:  How much does your body fat percentage and life style habits change from normal day to day living to competition time?**

As many competitors do, I eat well all year round as I enjoy good food and feeling healthy and energised.  When it comes to competition my life becomes much more structured, weighing out my food and ensuring I cook ahead for the week, having ordered all my protein in advance in a bulk buy.

Spontaneity goes out the window and my meals are timed through the day to fit with work and training.  Food becomes more like a fuel to achieve an end result rather than considering it as something to enjoy.

I make my food from 12 weeks, gluten, dairy and sugar free.

**CJ:  How do you measure your progress in the lead up to a show?**

I submit my weight to my Coach every week and he will look at me to assess progress and then make any recommendations. I also like to do calliper body fat readings over 9 points of the body.

**CJ: How does your training routine change in lead up to a show?**

It's important not to go into prep with all guns blazing and using all your ammunition at once. At the start I will bring in a little cardio which can increase as needed throughout the prep process. I look in the mirror and see how my symmetry is looking, see if there is anything that needs more or less work leading up to the show. Last year all I trained were legs, back and shoulders! I completely reshaped my physique for the category I wanted to do.

**CJ: How often do you exercise per week and how long is each session generally?**

It can change for what my body needs and the improvements I need to make. Out of contest I like to do 4 weight sessions a week, a cardio and couple of interval sessions during the week. In contest prep, I add more daily cardio and weights can be 3-4 days per week, My weight sessions normally last about an hour, intervals about 20 minutes and cardio anywhere between 30-60 minutes.

**CJ: What nutrition changes do you make?**

I work on 6 meals a day, 2-3 hours apart. All prepared at home using low sodium seasonings, herbs and spices for flavour. I'm not really fazed by what some would call 'bland' food! When reducing sugars and other processed foods, I find I taste 'whole' food much more!

I stop using whey protein, opting for foods instead. I will ensure a good intake of BCAAs and glutamine though around my training sessions. Once a week, I'll go out for dinner for a 'treat', ensuring I stick to my gluten/dairy/sugar free concept. My water increases also to about 4 litres a day, which to be honest, I find that hardest part!

I will use concepts such as Carb Cycling in contest prep as it is very effective for me in reducing body fat.

**CJ: Can you describe what a typical eating plan will look like during prep time?**

Meal 1; whole eggs, egg white, chicken, oats
Meals 2; 3 & 4: Chicken/turkey, lots of veg and sweet potato
Meal 5: white fish, asparagus
Meal 6; Lean steak or beef mince and spinach

**CJ: How does this compare to a typical day eating off season?**

Meal 1; Oats and whey protein
Meal 2: chicken and Greek salad
Meal 3: Prawns and mixed seafood, vegetables,
Meal 4: chocolate rice cakes, peanut butter and oatcakes or protein shake and nuts
Meal 5: Salmon and roasted vegetables

**CJ: What helps you to stay focused and motivated when competing?**

It's important to remember not to expect your final result after the first few weeks!! I start at the beginning by writing down my goals, breaking them down into daily, weekly and monthly targets. A daily goal could be 'drink 4 litres water' or 'I will eat all my meals and complete my training program'. For the weekly goal, it could be, 'I will go out for my cheat meal and stick to my plan' or 'take weekly stats and progress pictures'.

Another important thing I also do is to look at the bigger picture of this year and next few years ahead. What do I want to work towards, in competing, business and family?

**CJ: How do you deal with post competition blues?**

I often book a trip for when the show is finished. Not only does it give you something to look forward to while training, but it's great to get away from the routine and take a well-deserved break. When a show is finished I make more time for friends and family, making sure they know how much I've appreciated their support. I also get straight back into training but do something different like a class, crossfit or dance. The surge of calories in the post-show feed give me a real boost in training a day or two later!

**CJ: How do you manage the off season and time in between competing?**

I try not to have too big an off season and gain lots of weight. I don't like how I look and it makes things much harder! I like to reassess my goals. If I'm planning on another show, then I'll work at putting together a new plan. If I'm not going into another show, I'll work at making my training fun and varied.

I love to also re introduce foods such as whey protein, fruit, nuts and so on, back to the diet. All the great nutritious foods that I don't use in contest prep.

**CJ: What is your number one Top Tip to anyone either interested in competing or currently in training for a show?**

I would do your research. Go watch different shows, learn the criteria and different style of shows. Some are more pageant like and some a bit more serious on physique. Different Federations in different countries look for certain things and it pays to know what you are working for so your prep isn't wasted.

**CJ: If someone wants to train but not compete what would you advise?**

Still set yourself challenges and goals. Fitness, health and wellbeing doesn't end after a summer or after going through a transformation. As long as you're alive you can test and push the body to achieve strength, endurance and power. You will benefit in all areas of your life when you are fit, with a desire to achieve.

Health and fitness doesn't end at the end of your gym session, it's a lifelong journey that will have ups and downs, highs and lows, victories and defeats. It's how you overcome and drive forward, how you pick yourself up that will always make you a winner.

**Competition history**

Since starting the competing circuit I have achieved:
2011:
Musclemania Fitness England
- Bikini Model 1st Place
- Fitness Model 1st Place
Musclemania Fitness Britain Championships
- Bikini Model 1st
-Fitness Model 1st
Overall Champion
Musclemania Fitness Europe championships
- Bikini Model 1st
2012:
UKBFF Kent Klassic qualifier 2nd
UKBFF British Finals 4th
2013:
WBFF Denmark:
Bikini Diva 1st AWARDED PRO CARD
Fitness Diva 2nd
August 2013:

Qualified for Pro League for World Championships in Las Vegas. My pro debut and first international competition.

**CJ: Out of all of these, is there one standout memory?**

Winning my first show when my only goal was just to take one step on stage.

Check out www.onpointtraining.co.uk to learn more about Sian.

# Zöe Daly

When you first see Zöe you cannot help but notice that she is stunning, she has an amazing figure, gorgeous long blonde hair and a bright smile on her face. It is her beauty on the inside though that shines through and she is physically and spiritually simply stunning. Zöe is extremely down to earth, is extremely grounded and has a big heart that just loves to help others.

I remember the first time I saw Zöe was actually in the gym training and I admired her enthusiasm and focus. She trains hard and smart and was still smiling as she pushed through every last rep!

Interviewing Zöe was so much fun, she is very open and honest and it was like grabbing coffee with an old friend.

Zöe is an ambassador for health and fitness, a BSc sponsored athlete and an IFBB Champion, here she shares her story.

**CJ: Tell me more about how you got into competing?**

I had always been active as a child, I come from a fit family and when I was younger I used to rollerblade and out skate the boys at the skate park!

My passion was fitness was always there yet I did lose it a little in the terrible teenage years and in my early 20's I rediscovered my passion and started going to the gym. I used to call myself a cardio queen, I used to do a lot of classes especially BodyAttack and BodyPump was my version of weight training. It was a lot of fun.

In 2007 I started to get a lot of comments from people asking me when I was competing and I had absolutely no idea what they were talking about!

I became a PT in 2008 and started to learn more about what was involved with competing as a Fitness Model yet I was not ready at that time emotionally and it took me until 2010 to decide that I was ready.

**CJ: So did you feel that in 2010 you knew enough to get you going?**

No I had not watched a competition before plus I didn't do any prep. I just decided to go for it. My first show was the ANB Sydney Physique Titles on May 23rd which was also my birthday and I thought let's do this! It was kind of a birthday present to me and symbolic of overcoming emotionally instability I had dealt with for years. I thought yes I am in a good place, I can do this. I had no coach and did not prep, I just went for it.

**CJ: Wow, that's massive and would be incredibly daunting to a lot of others**

I believe that for your first show you just have to get up there and go do it, you learn so much, it's like on the job training. I was ready physically and I feel that you don't need to invest a lot of money employing someone to get you there, but hey if you want to that's fine as well. For me it was more that I knew I was going to do this, I was terrified about being on stage yet I knew I needed to do it to overcome that fear.

**CJ: Good on you, was this the deciding factor to compete?**

Well actually in the past I have done a lot of self-sabotage and I actually thought I would talk myself out of it. To be honest it was not about anything else other than a personal triumph and I am so glad I took the plunge. Who knows if I had not chosen to do this then I could have had another bad day where I felt totally overwhelmed and carried on in the same cycle. I decided to change the record!

**CJ: So tell me about your first show**

Well I had no idea what to expect, I just had a regular spray tan with a normal coat that would have looked great at the beach yet compared to the other girls I was reflective! I didn't have my hair or make up done, I was wearing a Seafolly bikini that I had actually brought for the beach plus I didn't have the classic clear heels that everyone else was wearing. You know what though, it didn't matter, I just got up and had a crack. I didn't even know how to pose!

**CJ: How were you feeling standing on stage next to the other girls?**

It was completely nerve wracking, a lot of them were seasoned competitors who were talking about travelling up and down the coast doing the other shows during that season. Even though it was actually quite intimidating it was also so much fun. I had my partner and parents there to watch me which was really special and after that day I never looked back, it became addictive!

**CJ: So how did you go?**

I actually placed 3rd out of over 30 girls which was exceptional – I would have been happy even if I had not placed because I did it, I got up there and did this thing that I never thought I could do.

**CJ: How did this make you feel?**

Exhilarated and on top of the world! Without sounding too cliché, it really did. I had a massive smile on my face which made my cheeks hurt! It was fantastic.

**CJ: Can you remember how you felt when you woke up on the morning of the show though? Most people celebrate their birthday by having a party and you were competing!**

It was like a double whammy, I was excited by the fact it was my birthday plus I just couldn't wait to get there, yet I was full of nerves with feelings of should I do this! It was a similar feeling to when I went skydiving, I was so psyched up and before I could talk myself out of doing it, I was actually jumping out of the plane!

**CJ: Clearly you got hooked on competing and not skydiving! When did you next compete after the ANB Sydney show?**

I kept going, I competed in 10 shows from May 2010 right up to the Arnolds in March 2012. I didn't have an off season in between shows as I don't really live the on/off season mentality; however I do realise the importance of a rest or down time.

After the Sydney show, I was on stage two weeks later in the ANB Asia Pacific in the Gold Coast which was a gigantic and phenomenal experience.

**CJ: That's a big step up, how did that show compare to your first?**

The Asia Pacific is massive, there were over 40 girls on stage that day and I actually had a moment of freak out, I went completely blank on stage and actually ran off crying.

**CJ: That must have been heartbreaking, what happened?**

We had to do a routine and in all honesty I am not a performer. Even though I did a routine before and knew what to expect, it was a whole new ball game. I was on stage and my mind just went blank, I literally froze and my immediate reaction was to run off.

## CJ: Did you get back on?

I was so upset and luckily my partner jumped up and gave me a massive hug and I went back out. Saying that though I was still upset at such a big stuff up and I thought it was all over yet I placed 4th out of over 40 girls. This was so incredible and was back in the day when all the sports models were placed in the same category and there was no advantage.

## CJ: Where did you go from there?

After this I flew to Melbourne to compete in the INBA All Female Classic and I placed 2nd in this show which was awesome, I was so happy that I was able to get back on stage as well as overcome external pressures that could have stopped me getting on the plane, let alone on stage!

As I was doing really well it become more addictive as I loved the feeling of being on stage and this is why I kept doing it. I was just having fun plus I also wanted to try out all the different federations to see which one my physique suited best.

## CJ: When you were prepping for these shows did you find it hard to balance work with training and dieting?

Well no, not really. At the time I was selling prestige cars and was lucky enough to be driving around in Mercedes and Porsche cars all day, I used to race and am a total rev-head!

So I loved my job and I was so pumped up on the adrenalin of having a goal to work to. Plus I chose to compete about a month prior to the actual show as I was already in the shape I needed to be in.

**CJ: As you started to compete in more shows what did you find that you enjoyed most about it?**

Pretty much everything, competing has given me so much ambition in every aspect of my life and has been such a positive influence.

As a child I was a high achiever and found I excelled in everything yet I think I actually burnt out, got over it all and became a rebel in the troubled teenage years I mentioned before. This went on into my early 20's and my life became all about partying every weekend and I really lost my sense of direction. I was floating through life without a purpose and this was extremely stressful for me, it created a lot of anxiety. Competing has created order and brought back the sense of purpose I needed in my life that I had as a child and given me inner contentment.

I have also met so many likeminded beautiful people who all have different stories as to what has brought them to compete yet we all share a love for being healthy and fit.

**CJ: It is definitely the people you meet and the adventures you have that make this sport so rewarding. Zöe, your biggest adventure to date has been going to the states to compete in the Arnolds, tell me about this.**

It was a true honour to represent Australia on an IFBB stage, it really was a dream come true and looking back on it, I learnt so much from that experience. I won the IFBB Nationals and got the invite to go to the Arnolds.

Even though this was a phenomenal opportunity in a sense though it did turn out to be quite a negative experience for me as I got quite ill on the plane to the states and there were stressful situations to overcome before I left yet I remained determined and focused on my goals.

**CJ:  So you got to the States, how did the Arnolds go?**

The 3 days leading up to the show where I should have been excited and relaxing I was in bed sick, I think my body went into shutdown mode and I remember going through endless boxes of tissues blowing my nose!  I had to get on stage in a bikini in front of thousands of people, get my hair and makeup done when all I wanted to do was to be in bed.  I got up there purely because I had this inner strength to prove to myself and others that I could do it.  Plus my beautiful parents had flown all the way from Sydney to be there just to watch me.  I refused to be a quitter and whilst that may seem negative I evolved so much from this one experience plus I got to represent my country on an international stage!

I truly believe everything happens for a reason and I became such a stronger person after this.

**CJ:  And after the show did you rest and recuperate?**

After the Arnolds we went to New York and there was literally chocolate and carbs everywhere!  Because I was such a wreck from the physical and emotional stresses I had been through, I literally let go and collapsed in a ball.  I shut myself away in the hotel for two days and ate crap.  I should have been having the time of my life yet I was a complete and utter mess.

**CJ:  Wow that is serious, plus combined with normal post comp blues must have been tough, how did you come back from that?**

I have experienced post comp blues nearly every time and this one went on for months.  I remember when I got back to Australia I actually had to go to Filex to represent my sponsors.  When I left for the Arnolds I was 9% body fat, when I got back I had gained 5kg, I didn't recognise myself and none of my clothes fit me.  Whilst most of this was fluid I had never weighed that much in my life and I felt horrendous.  I totally lost myself I stopped working as much, as I didn't want to face people so this impacted me financially.  I literally lost my confidence and withdrew from life.

I reached the point where I could not go any lower and it was at this point that I decided no, I need to take back control of my life. I started being kind to my body, began exercising and loving training again and eating healthy. It was certainly a process though to get back to a happy place mentally and I became my own trainer.

**CJ: So as a trainer, do you listen to your own advice?**

I listen to my body and believe in holistic nutrition - I eat everything now, within reason. Where in the past I had other PT's put me on restrictive ketosis diets I now eat carbohydrates and do not avoid foods. I feel happier, healthier and am giving myself more rest. I have found balance to my life.

**CJ: Not only do you train yourself but you also are a personal trainer and inspiration to so many others.**

Thank you. Yes I have clients all around the world and I feel like I have found my purpose again. After losing it for so long, it was so frustrating and now that I have got it back, I really love what I do.

Being on stage is great as it has helped me find my purpose which is to help other people.

**CJ: Can you tell me more about your exercise and nutrition philosophies?**

I don't believe in overtraining, in the past it was not uncommon for me to train twice a day and this actually led to injury which I have recently had to go through rehab for. I now listen to my body and will mix it up, I do yoga as well as weight training and do not do excessive cardio.

I work to an equilibrium mindset and will cycle workouts plus do split routines to avoid repetitive stress on the body.

In terms of eating this again is about balance and although I generally don't eat a lot of dairy should I get cravings then I will eat a small bit of cheese. If I want something I will have it, I don't have cheat meals as I think these can lead to binge days!

**CJ: So does your body fat percentage and lifestyle change a lot from day to day living to competition time?**

I am always close to competition physique, I am quite athletic and have always been a little fanatical, some may even say obsessive yet when I do something I do it properly.

**CJ: What advice would you give to someone thinking about competing?**

Just go for it. If you have the desire, then pursue it. You don't need to have a coach or be perfect as you will improve in all aspects of your life, not just physically. What you will learn from the experience itself is invaluable. Just enjoy and absorb everything.

You also cannot have any doubt, if you do then you are not in the right frame of mind. You need the fire in your belly, you will have this when you are mentally in the right place and this is what gives you a champion mindset.

**CJ: And if someone was unsure about competing and wanted to work towards a goal what would you recommend?**

Choose a goal such as a photoshoot and create a game plan to get you there as this will give you the focus and show you the way. Find something that inspires you.

**CJ: Do you have any role models that you look to for inspiration?**

I love Jamie Eason and Andrea Brazier. I also admire Jennifer Nicole Lee as she is very business savvy. Women who are strong with a beautiful heart inspire me, plus I will also look at old comp photos from time to time.

**CJ: You have had an amazing journey so far, you must be very proud of yourself?**

I am proud of everything I have gone through and everything I have overcome to get me here. I feel that I have gone through this to help others, I have knowledge and experience that can helps others overcome their obstacles and this is what I am driven to do.

**CJ: And your biggest highlight so far?**

One of my biggest achievements in my fitness modelling career was certainly representing Australia on the World stage at the Arnolds yet it was my most recent competition (WBFF Worlds 2013) where I earned my pro card that I am most proud of.

**CJ: Yes that is an outstanding achievement and one you worked so hard for, tell me more about the months leading up to that show.**

With this competition I kept it quiet and only those closest to me knew that I was getting back up on stage as I did not want to experience the same external pressures that had accompanied me during other comp preps. I was in great shape about 4 months prior to the comp and preparation was going really well when one day I woke up in pain with a bulging disc in my lower back.

**CJ: This is a serious injury, how did that impact your mental focus as well as your physical prep?**

Initially I was devastated as all the specialists I saw were telling me there would no way I could compete and I was unable to train. This could have really rocked me yet instead I chose to put all my energy into my business and I found that by sharing my situation with Clients was the best thing I could have done. The energy, love and support I received through the interaction on a daily basis with my clients, some of whom had gone through similar experiences was overwhelming and really enabled me to push through and continue to drive towards my goal.

**CJ: So were you still focused on competing?**

To be honest, not really, I was still doing what I needed to do to get there yet my full focus was on working with my clients and I believe that the energy I gave to them truly did come back to me tenfold to be able to persevere with getting to the worlds. By focusing more on my business and letting the comp prep happen naturally I found that I was a lot more relaxed, I was more balanced and I was actually really excited about getting to Vegas.

**CJ: So apart from the change of mind set was there anything else that allowed you to bring an improved package to stage?**

I have learnt so much about how my body responds to nutritional changes, I have increased my carbohydrate content substantially to what I used to have and am able to maintain a low bodyfat% whilst improving muscularity plus I have endless energy and full mental clarity! I cannot emphasise enough the power of eating carbs, protein and fats at every meal. By the time it came to leave for Vegas I was ready for stage.

**CJ: Tell me more about the whole trip:**

The whole experience was amazing and I met so many lovely people along the way plus have made some lifelong friendships with other competitors. From the start I decided to really indulge and treat myself so booked an amazing apartment and organised chauffeured limousines so I could really just concentrate on the task in hand. I arrived about a week out and rested up for a few days pre comp and then on the day whilst I was nervous about walking out on stage again after 18 months I felt confident in the package I was bringing. My body felt good – I have learnt to be in tune with what I need and can adapt the prep process to ensure that I feel energised rather than drained and tired. This really helps to get you on stage looking your best so you really shine.

**CJ: In the pictures of your performance you really do look like you're shining and happy. Plus your snow bunny costume was so cute!**

Ha (laughs) yes I chose to do something different that was cute and fun and represented what I am all about. The costume was truly made with love and stood out from the crowd.

**CJ: How was the atmosphere and interaction with the other competitors?**

It was different to what I have experienced before, everyone was so supportive of each other and we helped one another through small backstage crises – one girl's bikini broke so we found her a safety pin, I provided the rice cakes and peanut butter, you know the normal stuff. I met great people through the camaraderie and support backstage and formed close friendships.

**CJ: So the actual competition was on the Friday and you had to go back on the Saturday to get the results – how did it feel when you were called out you know you received your pro card?**

We were told that the top 3 girls from each category would receive the pro card so I knew if I could get a good placing then I would also get this. When they called my name as for 2nd place I was ecstatic, it was truly an overwhelming feeling of pride, accomplishment and made all the stress of the last few months disappear. Every hurdle has always proven to enable me to grow, to become stronger and come back fighting. When I received the official documentation to say I was now a pro I felt like I was walking on air.

**CJ: Yes I bet – how did you spend the rest of your trip post comp?**

We had a couple of days to go shopping plus head to Venice Beach before we had to fly back. I had my first session as a pro in Gold's Gym! I was so happy and buzzing from the show – it's a shame I couldn't stay longer! We just started to unwind when we had to leave.

**CJ: So how has life been since you returned?**

Life has been extremely busy since I have been back; I have been working on my business and now have clients in 13 countries around the world plus have prepped 5 girls for comps who have all placed in the top 5 in the recent season of shows. I prepped them the same way as I get ready, which is holistically and this ensures you feel good throughout the prep and are not depleted and dehydrated on stage.

I am also working on updating my website, expanding it to include testimonials and integrate the other new opportunities I will be working on to expand the Zöe Daly brand.

Plus of course there is always my own training and nutrition which I have to ensure remains a priority.

**CJ: What is next for you Zöe?**

I'm focused on continuing to grow my business and be able to help as many people around the world as I can. I will be taking on some new opportunities that have come my way and of course I will making my pro debut and competing to win a pro world title – the details of this comp will be kept quiet though!

**CJ: Yes of course! Zöe, thank you so much for your time, your honesty and for your inspiration. Do you have any final comments or advise how people can contact you?**

I am Australia's only WBFF Pro Fitness Model, Australian & International Champion. I am also a Poliquin Bio-Sig Practitioner & Nutrition student.

I am a Lifestyle Coach and have clients in 15 different countries around the world! My goal by 2014 is to be in 20 countries and by 2015, 50! I absolutely love what I do, helping others is the most rewarding career on this planet.

For information on my online Lifestyle Packages please visit my website www.zöedaly.com

## Competition History

**2010** ANB Sydney Physique Championships- May 23rd- Sports Model- 3rd Place

**2010** ANB Asia Pacific International (Gold Coast)-May 29th - Sports Model- 4th Place

**2010** INBA All Female Classic (Melbourne) - July 10th –Sports Model- 2nd Place

**2010** INBA NSW State Titles-September 26th – Sports Model- 1st Place

**2010** IFBB Australian National Titles -October 23rd- Bikini- 3rd Place

**2010** IFBB NSW State Titles- October 23rd- Bikini- 1st Place

**2011** Asia Pacific International Fitness Model Championships (GC)- June 13th - Fitness Model- 1st Place

**2011** IFBB Australian National Titles – October 15th- Bikini- 1st Place

**2011** IFBB NSW State Titles- October 15th- Bikini- 1st Place

**2012** Arnold's Sports Festival- March 1st, Columbus OH, USA -
Top 15 Finalist: Bikini

**2013** WBFF WORLD TITLES -August 23rd 2013. Las Vegas USA -
2nd Place Diva Fitness Model  PRO STATUS EARNED

# *Next Step*

So are you now inspired to compete? Each of the beautiful ladies who have shared their stories has definitely revealed their little secrets to help you on your way. So where to go from here?

First find a reputable coach and organise a meeting with them to chat about how they can help you. I also highly recommend speaking to other girls they have got ready and learn about the process through their eyes. Your coach will also discuss your choice of category as well as which federation to compete in. From here you will then be able to set your goal and make the plan for the incredible journey you are about to undertake.

Over the next couple of pages you will find my top tips that will assist you during your prep and on competition day plus information on the two main federations in Australia.

I cannot express enough my joy and excitement for you and remember it's not about winning the first place trophy. You have already won by just doing it, everything else is a bonus.

Good luck and see you on stage!

CJ

THE NAKED WARRIOR

# CJ's Top Tips

## During Your Prep

- Create a vision board or visual reminders of your goal to help with motivation
- Try to minimise social functions or travel as this can disrupt training routine
- Tell those around you what you are doing and why so they can help support you
- Go watch a competition so you can become familiar with what to expect when it's your turn
- Do speak to other competitors to learn their experiences
- Choose one coach and one program to follow - too many opinions causes confusion
- Buy your heels early in the process and get comfortable walking in them
- Start practising posing in front of the mirror. Do this as soon as you can - do not leave it to last minute. You need to be pose fit to maintain poses comfortable on stage even when fatigued - plus don't forget to smile!
- If you have to complete a routine then choose your music, choreograph a routine and practise this too. Your coach will be able to help with this.
- Get your posing bikini and outfits organised asap so you can get what you want and then it's one less thing to worry about.
- Always prepare your own meals and take them with you - eating out during comp prep can become difficult as you are not always in control of what is being added.
- Enjoy the process and keep a journal to record how you feel as well as what changes you are making physically. This can then be used as a reference tool for future competitions.

## Competition Day

It is best to chat to the competition organiser a few weeks prior to competition day to find out how the day will run as well as what your expected time to be on stage is. Always allow yourself plenty of time to get to the venue and you want to be backstage at least 30 minutes before your category is up.

Your coach will talk to you about how to prepare for the day as well as what to take with you. Below is a list of items that I generally take with me:-

- Copy of competition entry forms
- Federation membership details
- Running order sheet
- Music for routine if doing one
- Posing costume and outfits you may need to wear
- Towel
- Tape
- Wet wipes
- Make up/Hair accessories
- Spare bikini
- Food/Protein/Water
- Change of clothes for after the show
- Mobile & Ipod
- Resistance bands or hand weights for pump up

# THANK YOU

This book would not have been possible if it wasn't for the gorgeous girls featured inside so a huge thank you to everyone who shared their story. It is incredibly honouring to know that each and every one of you wanted to help me on my mission to open the competitor world up to more fearless females who are driven to try something new.

Thank you to you, the reader for having the curiosity and tenacity to take a leap of faith to empower yourself and find out what you are truly capable of.

Finally my heartfelt gratitude to everyone in my life who has provided the support, encouragement, education and reality checks that I have needed to get through each season of competing as well as helping to bring this book together.

Photo Credits

Dallas Olsen Photography
Glenn Marsden Photography
Toby Harrison Photography
Mariya Mova Photography
Andrew K Photography

Printed in Great Britain
by Amazon